THE DANISH

Michael Palmer

THE DANISH NOTEBOOK

Michael Palmer

Nightboat Books
New York

ISBN: 978-1-64362-123-4

Published by agreement with New Directions
Publishing Corporation.

Design and typesetting by Rissa Hochberger
Typeset in Kazimir

Cataloging-in-publication data is available
from the Library of Congress

Nightboat Books
New York
www.nightboat.org

....

The Danish Notebook begins as a letter, with Palmer writing, "Dear Iselin, you asked me to connect the dots," but not really: it begins with an epigraph from Edmond Jabès describing the sun as a girl "nobody has ever discovered." From this description of the sun-as-girl, Palmer describes himself as a young boy "sitting on the floor of a house, connecting the dots of a house."

We are immediately invited into a literary community, and in particular the intimate relationship between an author and publisher ("Iselin" being Iselin C. Hermann, a Danish novelist who once worked in the offices of the press that published Palmer's books in Denmark).

We are also immediately initiated into a series of notations that set up the book as a whole: not really a diary, a *real* "notebook," containing incidental notes, stories, quotes from various texts, a travelogue, and all of it threaded through with initial letter to Iselin. Notes: the sun as a girl, the sun inside Palmer's own book *Sun,* as well as the entry for "sun" in *Brøndum's Encyclopedia,* which Palmer has been commissioned to write. Palmer attempts (and fails) to write the entry throughout the writing of "the Danish book," the work Palmer has been commissioned to write as part of a series of notebook works from poets around the world. Rosmarie Waldrop has finished hers, she tells Palmer at a party. Palmer, for his part, worries throughout the book about his ability to finish it; as a model, he thinks about the work of Rosmarie's husband Keith, who has himself written a series of notebook-like works similar to what Palmer wishes he could attempt. And of course: this very book in which these words appear is testament he *did* actually finish "the Danish notebook."

So the book he writes is a divination for a book not yet written, describes failed encounters, near misses, abandoned assignments, missing diary entries (Palmer habitually makes entries for Leap Days but mysteriously misses the entry for one Leap Year —why?), and throughout, the text is punctuated—interrupted?—by notes Palmer is making for one of his many collaborations with Margaret Jenkins, this one for a dance called "Fault," inspired by the multiple fault lines which run through Palmer's hometown of San Francisco.

Besides the Waldrops, Palmer visits French poet Claude Royet-Journoud, searches for painter Jens Birkemose, discusses Merce Cunningham, obsesses over André Breton, and wanders the streets of Paris in a Surrealist *dérive* with poet Norma Cole, describing to her a long ago love affair, about which the reader— and Palmer himself it seems—is left somewhat unclear ever really took place. In that sense, it is a book of community, of encounters.

As much a work of choreography as prose, or perhaps even as much of of those children's dot-to-dot books as choreography, the modular form of the notebook undoes a sense of narrative or dramatic structure, while at the same time gesturing toward a larger body of literature—Keith Waldrop's *Garden of Effort,* Breton's *Nadja,* Palmer's own *Sun,* as well as the community of writers—Iselin, Rosmarie, Paul Auster, Georges Bataille, others—that makes writing happen.

"The dialogue between the near and the far. How the center empties as details accumulate," writes Palmer, as days pass in the notebook, "How the absent reappears, and the present..." He remembers his former trips to Paris, he travels to Hawaii with Jenkins and her dance company, recounts chance encounters—with Claude, with Jens, with Alexandra, the lover he had described to Norma—and those encounters seem as dreams: fixed neither in time nor space. Besides wondering if he's confused Alexandra with a character from Breton, he dreams of Claude in Hawaii, wonders how it is he actually met Jens Birkemose for the first time, tries throughout the book to remember the meaning of an English word he cannot find in any dictionary—a word whose root is French after all and which years later he cannot fathom why he hadn't known the meaning of immediately.

There is something of a divination the reader of the notebook must engage as they encounter the fragments and prose shards of memory, lanced through with fragments of choreographic notes from "Fault," shifts from first to third person and back, the pleading for more time to meet the deadline of Iselin, the reaming of memory for the meaning of the word "tasseography," the self-criticism for not being able to finish the entry for the word "sun" in the project of the surrealist encyclopedia—

The Danish Notebook enacts itself, becoming something more than Iselin asked for, more than *Brøndum's Encyclopedia* would have been able to contain. In its *dérive* through San Francisco, Boston, Sonoma, and Hawaii, it connects these dots into a picture wholly unexpected, deeply personal, richly textured, and with the fine and ordinary detail of any life.

And so does he finally figure out what "tasseography" means?

Well, as he began with Jabès, he ends with a quote and a photo. The quote is from Keith Waldrop's *Garden of Effort*, which has carried in his hand throughout his wandering: "These words/on parole," a phrase which to the translator or the francophone will carry *double entendre: parole*, in French, being another word for "word," besides the more common *mot, parole* being a certain type of "word" at any rate: referring to the act of "giving one's word," also the term for song lyrics—artistic connotation in French, carceral connotation in English, apt for the fault lines between language and experience the notebook reveals. The picture is the author photo in the original publication: a selfie before selfies, Palmer stands in front of a vanity mirror. He holds an analog shuttered camera up to his eye and snaps. The flash has gone off so the part of Palmer that is visible is his body. Rather than a face there is only a flash of bright light, the sun, or rather than the thing itself, its trace, its remnants of light.

Kazim Ali
San Diego
2021

THE DANISH NOTEBOOK

"The sun," noted Reb Gabbar, "is a flaming hoop which a little girl trundles around the earth. Nobody has ever discovered the child even though she plays in broad daylight."

Edmond Jabès tr. Rosmarie Waldrop,
Return to the Book

Dear Iselin,

You ask me to connect the dots. You ask whether I remember the "old childhood drawings" where you connected the dots until a figure appeared. I remember connecting the dots; I remember the dragon that appeared, the angel that appeared. A winged horse once, a small wooden house. I remember sitting on the floor in a house, connecting the dots of a wooden house. Sitting on a coco rug on the tile floor of a house, my grandfather's house. Connecting the dots of a wooden house, a dragon with an enormous tail, a horse with wings outspread. But I remember as well refusing once in a while to connect the dots in their numerical order, choosing instead to make a random pattern, with lines crossing other lines.

And you ask about the sun. You remind me that I never wrote about the sun for *Brøndum's Encyclopedia*, and I realize that I know nothing about the sun. I remember it less well than the black, angular purse you were carrying that day we visited the press in Nansensgade. The day you asked whether I knew a French poet named Claude Royet-Journoud. Yesterday I received a letter from Claude, saying that a book of mine published in France, *Cites*, a collaboration with the painter Micaëla Henich, had been reviewed on "France-Culture." I don't believe I've ever had a book of mine reviewed on radio here.

Soleil noir, soleil acéphale.

Mean distance from the earth: about 150 million kilometers. Diameter: approximately 1,390,000 kilometers. Mass: about 330,000 times that of the earth. We'll have to do better than that, of course.

There is, by the way, no sun today. It's a Wednesday in late February. Wind and rain have been blowing in from the west, off the

Pacific, for several days, and we've hardly seen the sun at all. It is the 28th, normally the last day of February, but I see that this is a leap year. I will have an extra day this year to attempt to connect the dots. To consider the sun, the question of the sun:

We sat on the cliff-head
before twin suns.

At the same time, the question of "fault." I am working on a new, evening-length dance piece with Margaret Jenkins and her company. Its title is "Fault." This city, in which I live, is built on a network of faults. These have the capacity, under certain conditions, to destroy the city. Seismologists and fault readers attempt to connect up the dots, to determine where and when an "event" (for so it's called) will happen next. In Prague last spring, people spoke of the perilous transition from Soviet occupation to independence and free-market capitalism. Several times I heard or read the expression, "It's like crossing a series of fault lines."

Today's mail just arrived. In it, another letter from Claude, containing a postcard designed by him, a representation of what I will call, for now, "the sun." It is postmarked 24 dec 1995, that is, a little over two months ago.

I once thought I should find a form for this little book you have asked for, but now it seems to me that unformed would be better, a book at fault. Displaced. I accepted your invitation because it seems an impossible thing for me to do, against my nature as a writer. Of course one should never have such a nature. If you discover that you do, you must erase it, as violently as possible. *Coup de torchon.* Clean slate. One of our cats, the apricot-colored one, is sleeping on the computer as I write this. He doesn't give a shit one way or the other. As long as the machine stays warm.

"...following an arc that ultimately has no tangent." (Deleuze, *Le Pli*).

In the new dance, by the way, one section is titled "The Fold." It explores the possibility of endless movement, endless surfaces, the folds of clothing and the folds of the body, folds within the earth, folds and creases on the surface of a rock. Deleuze again, "The movement never stops."

One day recently, a professor of physics we have been consulting brought a piece of moonrock to the studio for us to look at. It was very small and very dark, like the sun. It was very small and very dark, like the sun.

The sun, which is missing from your encyclopedia:

An indefinite calculus
watches, writes and rewrites

......

So as a result of my failure to respond, there is a lacuna, a black hole, in your encyclopedia, where the sun was meant to go. I can at least direct your attention to the entry, "Sun," in the *Critical Dictionary*, edited by Georges Bataille. It is the only entry attributed to Zdenko Reich. I have never before come across this name. Is it a pseudonym? An anagram I cannot unravel? A joke - one of those fictions created from time to time by the *Documents* and the *Da Costa* groups? A note in my edition simply reads, "Zdenko Reich - Biographical details remain few; before publishing in *Documents* he was part of the *Grand Jeu* group..." The entry itself is an exemplary rendition of surrealist ethnography, where oneiric and scientific imagery, and the sacred and the profane, become indistinguishable. The sun itself is not the subject. Instead we are offered the festival of a solar cult in the *Hautes-Alpes*, dating from the early nineteenth century, a festival of dancing and omelettes, celebrating the sun's return. The omelette, the sun's likeness, draws the sun down, once again, to expend itself.

......

Leap Year Day: an invention of Julius Caesar's astronomer, Sosigenes, in 46 B.C.E. No sun today, but I am listening for the first time to some preliminary musical materials for the new dance work. They leave me in a state of uncertainty, as was perhaps intended, since I can't make out their origins in the world of sounds. Listening again, I think I hear electronically modified wind instruments in one section, high-pitched bells in the next, like rain, muffled and variously altered industrial sounds in the third and fourth, building to a state of profound disquiet.

In my notebook for Leap Year Day four years ago, I find no entry. The closest to it is the entry for March 3rd, which consists of a single word, "Tasseography," starred as if I should be certain to return to it. I can find the word in none of my dictionaries.

The entry for Leap Year Day, 1988, contains a note on the word "float" in one of my own earlier poems. Nearby are references to the deaths of Robert Duncan (Feb.3) and René Char (Feb. 19).

No entry for Leap Year Day, 1982. On the first day of the month, I had woken at 4:45 a.m. and recorded the following, "Dream this night about going to film "Ragtime" (I haven't seen) with C. We are shown to separate seats and mine faces away from the screen, or 3/4 away,

so that I must turn and look over my shoul-
der to see. I then change seats to one nearer
C, but in this one I can only see the film in a
reflection on a large column, mirror-surfaced
and decorated with Art Deco style flowers (so
that I can't tell whether the film itself is affect-
ing a "deco" style). I tell C I have to leave and
she is somewhat reluctant, finally agreeing (I
tell her, "This is insane."). The manager is per-
fectly agreeable when I go to him for a refund,
though instead of giving me my money back (C
doesn't want a refund for herself), he hands
me six tickets, good only at the "Sacramento
Street Theatres." He then explains where some
of these are ("There's one at 2nd and Market")
and I look at the yellow tickets which are
printed in the conventional way but also have
some handwritten instructions, the only one
which I can make out reading, "Doors never
to open at 4 p.m.." My only hesitation in leav-
ing the film is that many others are leaving as
well, apparently out of dissatisfaction, leading
me to think that either it is in fact interesting

or it is pseudo-literary and pretentious. When
I wake, Teresa Stratas singing Weil's "Youkali"
is running through my head."

The despair that invariably overwhelms me
when I "look back" in this manner:

In a certain way all this still exists
but the scene and the mirror no longer exist

At the break of dawn tomorrow, will I raise an
omelette to the sun?

......

Crows have suddenly appeared in the branches
of the trees up and down our street. Abrupt,

sharp auditory memory of the rustling wings
and the cries of the crows, nesting in the trees
above the Jewish cemetery in Prague.

European crow. Jackdaw. In Czech, *kafka*.

......

I've been thinking about dots. Two years ago,
in the intense heat of August, I was wander-
ing with a friend through the streets of Paris.
We crossed the Pont-Neuf to the Ile de La Cité
and entered the Place Dauphine.

......

I broke off the above some weeks ago, unable to continue, fearing that I would fall into novelistic language in telling what, after all, is a fairly simple story, but one that I had repressed from my memory for many years. Now, the heat today once again brings me back to it. I'll start again.

I've been thinking about the dots. Two years ago, in the intense heat of August, I was wandering with a friend, the poet Norma Cole, through the streets of Paris. We crossed the Pont-Neuf to the Ile de La Cité and entered the Place Dauphine. As we traversed the Place in the direction of the Rue de Harlay I was overcome with the kind of obscure emotion which, for me at least, often precedes the recollection of a vanished thought or experience. I turned to look over my right shoulder and recognized the weathered exterior of the Hotel Henri IV. We continued walking to a nearby cafe as the pieces of this memory rapidly reassembled themselves. I felt, quite literally, as if I were being drawn downward into a dream state where fiction and fact, imagination and recollection, could no longer be separated.

At the cafe, I offered to tell Norma of the incident, of which I had never previously spoken to anyone. Over thirty years before (had I in fact recently turned seventeen?), I was spending part of a summer in Paris and had met and become friendly with a young dancer from Hungary who was studying, perhaps as an apprentice dancer, at the Paris Opera Ballet. We were introduced by a mutual acquaintance, an American, who had met Alexandra while browsing through bookstalls on the Boulevard Saint Michel. We had dinner that evening, and over the next few days she introduced me to her small circle of friends, most of whom, like herself, were a year or two older than I. During the following weeks we spent as much time together as possible. I would pick her up after her classes, and we would wander around the city, visit museums, go to films and at night often listen to music in clubs (Bud Powell with his trio once, maybe at the Blue Note). On a narrow street in the sixth, she indicated an atelier where her grandfather, a composer, had lived for a number of years. French had become the second language in her home in Budapest. Thus it was to France part of her family had fled after the failed uprising of 1956.

On one of our walks, I pointed out to her the window of my room on the third floor of the Henri IV. Some days after that we were at a party where I was taken aside by two men with thick Hungarian accents. I was told that Alexandra was in immediate danger and would have to leave France. They could not say to what country she would be taken, and she herself did not yet know. She had asked to spend her last two nights with me at my hotel, and this had been agreed, provided I assured them that she would not leave the room until they came for her.

I think it was while lying awake the first night, after we had been taken to the hotel, that she asked, teasing, Why poetry? I had replied, with a pretentiousness that immediately embarrassed me, Because we're made of language. At my then obligatory question, Why dance - *Alors, pourquoi la danse* - she had laughed and answered, Because we're made of legs and arms!

I would go out for sandwiches, mineral water, beer, cigarettes in blue packets. She requested tangerines, a copy of *Aurélia*. Each evening we would smoke a little more from the small stash of pot given to me by a friend. We wondered what her new name and new country would be, what language would be spoken, whether she would be able to dance. The stained and peeling wallpaper depicted scenes along a broad river, figures in Levantine clothing, loading and unloading small sailing barks.

How sweat models the body.

The idea of a narrative, that, let's say, X and Y might have been; that to say something is possible, or possibly true, is to say that it is not necessarily false.

Very early on the morning of the third day, the same two men who had first approached me came for her. I watched from my window as they took her from the still darkened square to a waiting car.

In the same heat and the same month, I told the story to Norma as she ate ice cream and I drank a beer, a few hundred meters from where it had occurred. I felt it turning into fiction as I did so and wondered at this betrayal.

Returning to the United States, I wrote a tortuous version of it as a piece called "Autobiography 11." On December 2 of that same year, 1994, after completing the latest draft of "Autobiography 11," I came upon this passage in Mark Polizzotti's biography of André Breton:

"A kiss is soon forgotten," Breton had said elsewhere in "Soluble Fish," speaking of an amorous encounter in Place Dauphine - a square that always caused him an indefinable malaise. On the evening of October 6, it was the same Place Dauphine that Nadja led Breton to in a taxi. On the way she had offered her lips for the first time....

A footnote reads in part, "Breton later attributed this malaise to the realization that, for him, Place Dauphine was 'unmistakably the sex of Paris.'"

......

In the *Critical Dictionary*, "formless" (*l'informe*, better translated as "unformed"):

> A dictionary would begin as of the moment when it no longer provided the meanings of words but their tasks. In this way *formless* (sic) is not only an adjective having such and such a meaning, but a term serving to declassify, requiring in general that every thing should have a form....

......

I am leaving in a few weeks for Paris, and I have promised to tell this story to Claude, if he will agree to meet me at the Place Dauphine on May 23rd, Nadja's birthday. Then this little notebook will be done.

(A call from my French publisher. It seems that Emmanuel Hocquard's translation of my book, *Sun*, will appear in Paris during that same week.)

......

In Persian mystic poetry and folklore, the sun is a round-cheeked girl (*korshid*).

......

Parmenides' journey in the sun's chariot, accompanied by the daughters of Helios: crossing the divine threshold of night and day, he came to grasp "the unshakeable heart of well-rounded truth."

......

The Manichean sun god, known as the Third Messenger (*Neryosang*), who lives in the sun and sets the sun and moon in motion, creating the changes of the seasons.

......

Going back through my notebooks, I come upon the day of our first meeting, Iselin, when I agreed to write the entry for "Sun," and when you told me of the first encounter between Jens Birkemose and Claude:

23 sept 1993 / Copenhagen

At Brøndum Forlag today, Iselin Hermann ("forlagsredaktor") and I discover that Claude Royet-Journoud is an old mutual friend. She tells me the story of Claude's first meeting with Jens Birkemose (the painter who has provided illustrations for my Danish book, *An Alphabet Underground*), when both were living on the Rue du Dragon. Claude admired Jens's work but was shy about approaching him. Finally, after some weeks or months, encouraged by Jens's wife, he bought a large bouquet of flowers and rang the bell of the apartment of Jens and his wife. Jens opened the door and, upon seeing Claude, immediately grew deathly pale. Claude of course was terrified that he had somehow given offense and offered to leave immediately, but Jens said no. It turned out that the week before, in the street nearby, Jens had found a roll of film which he had immediately developed. It contained twenty-four pictures of Claude.

......

Iselin telling me today that Editions de Minuit sells (X) copies per year of a Beckett title in France. Brøndum sells (X divided by 10) of the bilingual edition in Denmark. The smallness of both figures astonishes me.

......

Later in the day, Bob Creeley tells me the story of his meeting Beckett, via their mutual publisher, John Calder, and his wife at that time, Bettina. An entire night spent in a cafe, with Beckett telling how he had looked for one word that might stand, upright, alone. As Bob put it, not, obviously, "The Word," nor even "a word," but "word," pure and simple.

Bob and I then talk about Michael Ondaatje, whose *The English Patient* I am reading here in Copenhagen for the first time. "All day they have shared the ampoules of morphine. To unthread the story out of him, Caravaggio travels within the code of signals."

I think about the collection of writings on poetics I edited many years ago, and its title, *Code of Signals*, part of a citation from Osip Mandelstam's "Conversation about Dante," "Poetic speech is a carpet fabric with a multitude of textile warps which differ one from the other only in the coloring of the performance, only in the musical score of the constantly changing directives of the instrumental code of signals." This seems to sit perfectly beside Ondaatje's usage.

......

As I am copying the above, I receive a call from the Brazilian Consul in San Francisco, himself a novelist. In the course of our conversation, he mentions to me that Bob Creeley is in Brazil and just spent an evening with Haroldo de Campos, one of the poets in Copenhagen with us that September. And Bob telling Haroldo that Bob and I have not seen each other since Copenhagen.

......

A letter arrives from Rosmarie Waldrop, wondering whether I have completed my "notes" for Denmark and telling of her anxiety about finishing on time. I reply that I have completed the notes for the notes but have not filled in all the words. Then I wonder when exactly is/was the deadline. But the work now wants May 23rd as its deadline.

......

There is a sixth century golden medallion from Mersina (ancient Turkey) in the Hermitage in St. Petersburg. It shows the emperor Constantine flanked by figures embodying the sun and the moon. Above the headdress of the sun, who is handing a crown to the emperor, there is a solar sign, an eight-pointed star. The emperor is larger than the sun, who is paying him homage.

......

The "sun game" of polo, played during the time of Akbar (1542-1605) with an ignited "sun ball."

......

From about the middle of the fourth century, it becomes permissible to depict Christ with a crown of sun rays, like the Roman emperors before him. Around the sixth century, such haloes begin to appear on portraits of Mary and other Christian saints. By Carolingian times, the pagan sun symbols have been entirely absorbed into the Christian tradition.

......

Robert Smithson's idea of "a surd map," that is, a map without a central logic.

......

Yesterday, for the new dance work with Margaret Jenkins ("Fault"), I wrote:

What do you see?

I see signs of movement in the leaves, the wind beginning to pick up.

What do you see?

I see a blind woman in a dark scarf and over-coat, tapping a path with her cane along a sidewalk bordered with snow.

From the window, what do you see?

I see the burned-out shell of a streetcar, frozen in mid-turn. I see children playing amid the debris, people gathered here and there in groups, some looking up and pointing, a few dogs wandering aimlessly.

And it occurs to me that this new work is about connecting the dots, above and below, about dance as a way of seeing rather than as, so often, something simply "to be seen."

......

A letter from Iselin, saying that she has been to Paris and has met with Claude, and that she too believes in deadlines.

......

Today, for the dance, I wrote:

What can you see?

I can see the winter sun, low and pale above the garden fence, a hawthorn without leaves, some bare fruit trees and vines of bittersweet, a sun-dial that's...

What do you see?

I can see what looks like a face. Maybe you can see it as well. A face half turned away, of a girl or a young woman, her hair drawn back tight, the way a dancer might wear it. I don't know what it means - maybe she's in the process of leaving, yet still undecided, hesitating for some reason. There is apprehension and, I think, sadness, but it's hard to say.

What did you see?

At noon, precisely, I saw the lights go out and the doors clang shut in the cafes and bookstores and souvenir shops around Old Town Square. I heard a single bell tolling in the turrets of Tyn Church. In the middle of the square, hundreds of young women with babies in carriages gathered at the statue of Jan Hus. The whole city, maybe the whole country, seemed to be in the streets. I saw a line of high school students in the old ghetto, chanting freedom slogans as they passed the synagogues.

......

Sun n. 1. A woman's bag for carrying keys, a wallet, and other personal items. 2. A small bag or pouch for carrying money. 3.A pocket-sized, usually paperbound, book.

......

If, otherwise, he were to write the episode of the Place Dauphine, it might appear thus:

And eyes: he is eyeless
A mirror sees for him

......

The death of Heiner Müller; death of Levinas.

......

Sun-disc between the thighs of an Aztec ter-
racotta figure.

......

I've found an old notebook fragment, "And here
in the Zero Quarter, below ground the sun is

shining, the stars are out, the..."

......

Iselin, I should explain my delay in return-
ing the contract for this book. I held it for a
month before signing it, frightened and dis-
abled by the nature of such a document, the
mystery of its linguistic transparency. Or do I
mean opacity? The curious thought that you
will agree to deliver a text, that there will be
words when you need them. Who can guaran-
tee this? And yet the thought of the project, of
the dots with lines extending between them
forming an angel's wing or a solar halo, grad-
ually lifted me from a period of drift and ano-
mie. In a room with a group of people soon
after sending off the contract, I found myself
standing with my hands outstretched, held
about eighteen inches apart. Someone asked,
"What are you doing?" Embarrassed - I had
momentarily forgotten there were others in

the room - I said, "That's the Denmark book."

......

Waimea, Hawaii. Arrived today at Kona airport with the dance company and drove up through the lava fields to our hotel in the hills near the base of the Mauna Kea volcano and within sight of Mauna Loa. Intense sun, but a landscape that absorbs the light into its blackness.

We attend the ceremonial benediction for a new grove of trees at the theater. A native Hawaiian woman performs the ceremony with simplicity and evident emotion. We speak afterwards. In response to my question she tells me that her first prayer called back her ancestors and greeted them. The second spoke to the nature of the place, the above and below, the four poles, dawn and dusk. I do not ask why she was frequently in tears throughout the ceremony.

At dinner I am introduced to the people who support the local theater. All are white, elaborately dressed and earnest about culture. I wonder how they will react to our performance on Friday. I wonder what I can possibly read to them next Monday. Halfway through dinner, the community chorus enters and sings selections from Gilbert and Sullivan, from Brigadoon and Kismet, a Billy Joel tune arranged for chorus, a series of saccharine contemporary madrigals. I can feel my brain beginning to wobble, a familiar prelude to a wave of depression.

Out for a walk after dark, I hear scattered dogs barking, a car with a bad muffler sputtering to a start, just before the rain begins. Scent of plumaria.

......

Waimea. The construction of entire new towns here in the hills, for the workers who will service the tourist hotels on the coast.

This afternoon, we traveled in a four-wheel drive truck through the lava fields of Mauna Loa and up to the top of Mauna Kea, 14,300 feet, where several astronomical observatories are located. Mauna Kea has not erupted since before the last ice age, but Mauna Loa's most recent flows date from 1986. We see them on the west side of the road, free of almost all vegetation, stretching toward the sea.

Two-thirds of the way up Mauna Kea, we stop to put on layers of sweaters and down clothing. The wind will reach fifty or more miles an hour, the temperature drop to thirty or forty degrees below zero. Ancient Hawaiians lived in caves high up on the sides of the volcano, where they would fashion arrows and tools from volcanic rock, for use and for barter.

At the summit, well beyond the cloud layer, is the world's clearest atmosphere. As the sun declines, a brilliant crescent moon in Venus appears, with Orion to the west over the ocean. The Comet Hyakutake is clearly visible below the handle of the Big Dipper, its tail not that sharply defined, perhaps due to the brightness of the moon. As the sky darkens further, myriad other constellations become visible, but as always I have trouble identifying all but the most obvious. I can see the dots of light, the countless suns, but I cannot connect them: Pegasus, Andromeda, Cassiopeia, Ursa Major and Ursa Minor, Draco, Pisces, Aquarius, Libra, Eridanus, Perseus, Leo, Hercules, Aquila, Coma Berenices, Cygnus, Vulpecula, Camelopardus, Auriga, Cetus, Delphinus, Lacerta...

......

From his room within sight of the Mauna Kea volcano, he sends a postcard of a tropical waterfall to two friends in Bordeaux. On it are nothing but the words, "Tristes Topiques?" On other cards, however, he writes vivid descriptions of his trip through the lava fields, the ascent of Mauna Kea, the surrounding craters, the sun setting over the Pacific, the view of Orion in the western sky (the shining belt, the sword, the two stars marking the shoulders), the patches of snow, the ferocity of the wind at the summit, the view of the comet beneath the Dipper's handle, the cluster of metallic observatories, the sight of Mauna Loa not far off, the difference between the two principle types of lava, the various flora that soon begin to spring up in the fissures of the lava (one, tiny, with bright orange flowers), the military base in the lava fields, established during World War II, the occasional helicopters, the physical hazards of ascending to 14,300 feet - how for example you must monitor your breathing - it is no longer purely autonomic, the wild sheep, goats and pigs, the various exotic trees and brilliantly plumed birds, the periodicity of the comet (it appears every 10,000 years), native artifacts to be found there (axheads and arrowheads, the ancient sleds discovered in the caves), the meaning of the mountains' names (Mauna Kea, "White Mountain," Mauna Loa, "Long Mountain"), the fact that the discoverer of the comet was an amateur Japanese astronomer, the many abstruse technical problems in constructing an observatory, the not unpleasant light-headedness at the summit, the changed pressure on the eyeballs which alters vision, the thickening of the blood as the body draws needed water from it at that altitude, thus the danger of dehydration, the enormous berms of iron oxide occasionally visible during the climb, the subtly shifting color spectrum as you ascend, the absolute clarity of the atmosphere, the sacred myths associated with the two volcanoes (the wars of the goddesses), the passion of our guide in offering us information, the special photographic plates which must be "baked" on site for the observatories, the fact that one successful photographic plate can provide an astronomer with as much as five years of information to investigate, the three deaths during the construction of the Japanese observatory (prayers and offerings had been made to Shinto gods at the start of construction, but none to the gods of the Hawaiian people), the environmental controversies that explode each time a new observatory is proposed, the bizarre, chalet-style building which houses the scientists well below the summit, the dangers of the road itself, on which people continue to die with regularity, and the fact that, at the summit, one's intelligence quotient is reduced by about 10%.

......

Yet to two friends in Bordeaux, he has written only the two words, followed by a question mark and the greeting, "Love, Michael," with the date at the upper right. Over the following days, he gradually comes to understand why.

......

In his notebook, on that same day, he writes, "I am, here, how many miles from Copenhagen? from San Francisco? from Paris?"

He writes, "My face a bright red from the wind on top of the volcano last night, and the intense glare of the lowering sun in the thin atmosphere."

The following day he writes, "In the window

of Waimea's Authentic Western Wear Shop, I see a T-shirt with a picture of palm trees and the lowering sun just above the horizon. For the Danish notebook, this would comprise part of the subsection: *Sun, as ornament to casual clothing.* I am suddenly reminded of how, north of San Diego, kids gather each day along the beaches at sunset, to watch the sun disappear, and to hoot and applaud appreciatively, almost as if it had never happened before or, at least, not in quite that way before."

"Sitting in Lanahila Park, I turn and see a woman riding by on a unicycle, her dog trotting beside her on a leash. Four cedars, four pines, five bushes of brunfelsia."

"Pen found on the table of a Waimea cafe, with name taped to it: Michelle Hotchkiss."

"'Banality of marigolds,' the man thinks, looking out the window of the cafe. Later, approaching the flowers in their border, he realizes that they are not marigolds, but some form of succulent he has never seen before. The shape of the flowers, however, and the gold and yellow hues, are virtually identical to those of marigolds."

He remembers the words of the guide, "And at this altitude, your lungs may suddenly begin to fill with water, and if they don't get you off the mountain immediately, you will drown."

......

He is four, maybe five years old. In the swirls of marble over the fireplace, the child sees the face of a woman with long, flowing dark hair. Years later, he would scan Pre-Raphaelite paintings for that same face and hair.

......

He reads that the dead are still dead in Srebrenica, the Black churches still burning in the South.

.

......

Perhaps, Iselin, what I am doing is entirely redundant. As I sit here in Waimea, reading Keith Waldrop's *The Locality Principle*, it occurs to me that he has written what I would like to write for this project - has in certain instances written beyond what I can offer. An example is the section entitled "Two Musicians," which I heard him read in San Francisco some weeks ago. The question of tuning. Its cover photo by Ben Watkins, who also did the cover of my book *At Passages*. On that same program Keith read from his recently published translation of Claude's *A Descriptive Method*.

......

This feeling of things beyond my abilities (as in reading *The English Patient*), a mixture of rapture and, inevitably, regret.

......

Life on the road - what I keep in my room: Japanese rice crackers wrapped in seaweed, grapes, bananas, dried fruit, single malt scotch, mineral water.

How this varies according to location. For example, in Paris the time before last, in my room at the Hotel des Grandes Ecoles: *clémentines*, bread and cheese, calvados, mineral water. A friend had brought me the *clémentines*.

And in Leningrad, 1990, whatever we could fit into our luggage, from a Helsinki supermarket, before our trip to the Finland Station: crackers, grains, dried soups, bottled water, fruit juices.

......

Did I mention solitude, which in traveling across multiple time zones seems to deepen and darken? I could only describe its taste by the dreams it provokes, their sharp, halluci-natory character. In Stockholm the first night, on the way to Russia, a dream of islands in the bay, their castles guarded by gates resem-bling mouths with enormous teeth. The cas-tles' mouths constantly opening and closing, under twin, nocturnal suns.

And that total solitude which stimulates memories and dreams of all the women you have ever been with, and those you've wanted to be with. The pure experience of loss, limit-less regret.

......

Tremor, 4 P.M., rolling through my hotel room, northeast to southwest, as I'm trying to take a brief nap.

......

Before the mirror, shaving, as he approaches
the age of his father the summer night he died.

......

Horse pulling a Bronze Age sun chariot, in
Trundholm, Denmark, bearing a sun disc gilded
on one side to represent the day-sun, while the
obverse, ungilded, represents the night-sun.
Rg Veda: "the horse of yonder sun, rising from
the water like the spark of life..."

......

A woman approaches me after last night's dance performance, holding a copy of *At Passages*. "Your poems are all so sad! Couldn't you write some happy poems? I'm too old for sad poems. When I was young, I read Edna St. Vincent Millay (she recites a few well-known lines). And Ogden Nash - I always liked Ogden Nash."

......

I had first thought to finish the Danish notebook on April 1st, All Fools Day, but it wasn't to be.

......

Reading in San Francisco last night, with Milosc, Snyder, Ginsberg, Thom Gunn, Adrienne Rich and several others before an intense, anticipatory crowd of 700-800 people, so different from the poetry reading as we otherwise experience it. How is the intimate voice heard in such a space? How is silence heard? My instinct was to read my quietest work.

......

The place where Levinas's ethics invariably founders: where "the Other" cannot be equated with "someone else"; where "the Face" is faceless.

......

When people ask me what I'm doing "these days," I reply that I'm working on a new dance piece and on my Danish notebook. I do not tell them that I don't know what these things are.

......

Or what "these days" are.

......

"Flesh-eating Virus Takes Another Life"

......

Cunningham's "Ocean" today, performed in Berkeley, a few days after Merce's 78th birthday ... watching Merce arrive at the theater, walking now so arthritically. His question to me of some years ago, asking whether it was a mistake to go on performing with the greatly reduced skills of old age. My reply (meant with complete sincerity), that he should continue to perform until he couldn't move at all, then perform some more.

The shift in the reception of his work in recent years. Now it has an almost classical feel, closer perhaps to Balanchine than to what we see in contemporary "modern

dance." Its pure, unapologetic sense of move-
ment as its own excuse for being.

......

The Tory culture of American *poésie officielle*.

......

I've felt death with me all day today, as some-
times happens, not as adversarial "Grim
Reaper" but as silent companion, even friend.
Present as I translated from the Russian all
morning, and then in the seat next to me in
an auditorium at Stanford University as I

listened to the sweet, Scots-inflected voice of Alec Finlay lecturing on his father's poetry garden not far from Edinburgh.

......

The lovers coupling on the walls of the sun temples at Khajuraho and Konarak.

......

At Sonoma State University today, I began my reading with my translation of Alexei Parshchikov's "Flight II," with its references to the Chernobyl disaster. Not realizing that it was the tenth anniversary of Chernobyl. At the time of the explosion, my wife and daughter and I were at the Fondation Royaumont outside Paris. Everyone gathered before the television and listened to the reports denying that any radioactivity was detectable in France:

At the start of the war of the worlds harsh wormwood's scent intensifies.
Preparing to set out, I was scraping bugs from the radiator when a new fire scorched half our lands, targeting, but missing us.

Gas station's ashes. Sea-foam and dust. Nothing around but this control panel with its eternal lies.
Was a horseman there, or was it sand scattered from the sky along the tide...

......

A brief visit to Boston, for the wedding of Bill Corbett's daughter. At lunch with Paul Auster and Siri Hustvedt before the wedding, I discuss the Danish notebook. I tell the story of Claude's first meeting with Jens. I mention that when Iselin first told it to me, I felt as though I might have read it previously, somewhere in Paul's work. I wonder whether Claude has already told him this story, but Paul says he's never heard it before.

......

On the television news in Boston, we hear of a relatively mild earthquake in the San Francisco region. Slippage along the Hayward Fault.

......

A brief letter from Claude today, mentioning a plant that he has had for more than ten years. How, a few nights ago, while he was reading at about one in the morning, he noticed that it had begun to flower for the first time.

......

In Aquitaine in the fourth century, a flaming sun-wheel rolls down a hillside.

......

My realization today that I have lost my awareness of words, single words as themselves, material elements, soundings. I have become too used to *using* them. Does this mean I've learned nothing at all from listening to Scelsi all these years?

......

For "Fault":

From there, what do you see?

In the window opposite I can see a table covered with artist's materials. A man enters. He goes briefly to the table, only to turn away suddenly, even violently, and hurry from the room.

What can you see now?

I'm looking at the diagram of a hand covered with writing in a language I don't know.

What do you see?

I see a stone, a large boulder suspended in the afternoon sky. Creases and folds criss-cross its surface. At its top, the ramparts and towers of a castle.

What do you see?

I see Cassiopeia, Cepheus, Draco, Ursa Major and Ursa Minor in the northern sky, Andromeda and Pisces in the east, Capricorn and Sagittarius at the ecliptic to the south.

......

Rehearsal of "Fault" tonight, for the preview performance just prior to my departure for France. The first half is almost ready, the second half not close.

To the text I add:

What do you see?

I see a young woman gazing at the comet below the handle of the Big Dipper. She is playing distractedly with the dark hair at the nape of her neck, curling it between her fingers.

......

Prehistoric sun images on the rock walls of the Dudumahan caves on the Kei Islands of eastern Indonesia: rayed circles, circled crosses, concentric circles, spoked circles with a smaller circle at the center, and various combinations of these forms.

......

Kazakhstan: the bronze feline coiled within solar rays.

......

Spider web: symbol of the sun god Sûrya's night garment in Hindu mythology. Woven by Ushas, the goddess of dawn.

......

Etruria: the winged boy with body and skin of a reptile, emerging from the sea.

......

Rereading the early entries for these notes, I find a comment on "Leap Year 1982." Of course, that was not a Leap Year. I should have been looking in my notes for 1984, where there is also no Leap Year Day entry.

Under February 11th: "'Forgive the world, however terrible it is.' William Bronk, *Costume as Metaphor*."

February 12th: "Now I know I would rather embrace the flaws."

February 14th: "Robert Duncan, 'The form is a revelation of the story.'"

February 15th: "LEC(RI)TURE, à Claude Royet-Journoud." (This apparently a work never realized.)

......

I arrive in Paris at 10:10 a.m.. On my *Carte d'Entrée*, under profession, I write *poète/professeur*, then cross out *professeur* and replace it with *traducteur*.

That evening I have dinner with the American painter Irving Petlin and his wife Sarah on the

Rue du Cardinal Lemoine. We talk about Claude, Ron Kitaj, Antonio Lopez, Leon Golub and many others. He mentions his recent portrait drawings of Susan Howe, Jacques Roubaud, Keith and Rosmarie. I leave about 10 p.m., taking the Rue Clovis up past the Panthéon and the Bibliothèque Sainte Geneviève. To my left, I see the Hôtel des Grands Hommes, where Breton stayed when he first came to Paris. Since my last visit they have put up a plaque, officially commemorating it as the site of the discovery of automatic writing by Breton and Soupault. Descending the Rue Soufflot toward the Boulevard Saint Michel, I hear snatches of conversations among young people standing around in small groups:

"I have absolutely no accent in German, but English is something else."

"The Socialists have all the money and the peasants - le Droit - have none."

Near the Rue Auguste Comte, at the edge of the Luxembourg Gardens, I see a kiosk advertising "Un Vampire de Brooklyn." It pleases me to walk along this street named for a man who believed that knowledge of the world arose from observation, one who held that the causes of phenomena and the nature of things-in-themselves are not knowable. It pleases me even more never to have read his six-volume *Cours de philosophie positive*. I imagine M. Comte as a vampire from Brooklyn. It begins to rain as I enter my apartment, very close to the Dome and the Rotonde. My bed lies under a Man Ray lithograph of a woman's heavily rouged lips hovering in a cloud-filled, crepuscular sky above a landscape. In the apartment, as I turn on the lights and wander around, I find other paintings and graphics by Matta, Bacon, Petlin, Seymour Rosofsky.

I attempt to phone Claude but only reach his *répondeur*. I leave a message, asking whether we are still to meet on the 23rd.

......

You cannot forget that you are *embodied*.

You cannot remember whether, at this corner, years before, you turned left or right.

......

I go to Irving's studio to begin to take notes on, and to "write toward," his *Seine Series*: the river at flood, two winters past; the bodies of the dead, afloat, October 17th, 1961; those "figures-which-are-not"; the sky escaping its frame.

"Paris is white." Edmond Jabès.

What is submerged
behind the liquid - flooded -
eye

"To bring together the expired space with its
origin and full self."

The dialogue between the near and the far.
How the center empties as details accumulate.
How the absent reapppears, and the present...

......

Paris dream: Claude and I are at the summit of
Mauna Kea in the early darkness, where I am
explaining to him the intricacies of the opti-
cal devices, the technical problems posed by

extreme fluctuations of temperature, violent winds, snow, and the unfiltered rays of the sun. We turn to leave, but our car and driver have departed. We can make out the lights of the car as it follows the winding road down.

......

An inventory of Irving's studio: erasers, boxes of pastels, brushes, paint daubs arrayed in a half-oval, pencils, pens, charcoal, chalk, push-pins, tubes of oils, sawhorses, notebooks, cans of fixative, jars, draughtman's triangle, masking tape, measuring tape, photographs, sketch pads, books, cassette tapes, radio/tape player, painting smock, scissors and tools, picnic knife (Opinel), film canisters, dusting brush, stapler, wine glass and water glass, pile of exhibition catalogues, two gooseneck lamps, resin bags, palette knives, rolls of sketching paper, dust-broom and canister, reading glasses, rubber bands, mirror, c.7" x 9", draughtman's T-square, large clips, chamois.

......

We go to see Robert Altman's *Kansas City* at the *Grande Action* on the Rue des Ecoles. I recognize a few musicians I know in the cast. Very good musicians, maybe better than the film which, itself, is better than people will think.

......

Dear Iselin,

I spoke with Claude by phone yesterday. Tomorrow, the 23rd, we will meet for the first time since last May, when I passed briefly through Paris after a stay in Prague.

......

Graffiti on the wall of the Eglise Sainte Geneviève, across the street from the Lycée Henri IV:

> Excelle dans l'art
> de ne rien faire

And to the right of it, hastily scribbled:

Luke
la main froide

......

Dear Iselin,

I picked up Claude at his apartment around noon today, where he showed me a suite of astonishing erotic drawings by Jens Birkemose, published last year by Brøndums in three volumes. We walked over to the Place Dauphine, and Claude offered a glass of champagne in honor of Nadja's birthday. I then told him, as I remembered it, the story you had told me of Claude's first meeting with Jens. He approved of this version but then proceeded to tell me the story as he remembered it.

After much hesitation, at the urging of Jens's wife he finally made an appointment to meet Jens. He doesn't recall whether he brought flowers, though he is certain that he brought along a copy of Keith Waldrop's *The Garden of Effort* as a gift. Their first meeting was very pleasant, with nothing out of the ordinary. A few weeks later, Jens discovered a canister of film that he had picked up from the sidewalks of the Boulevard Saint Germain some months before. He had brought it home, placed it on his desk, and forgotten about it. Opening the can, he found a roll of already developed film. On it, twenty-four images of Claude. He noticed that in one frame Claude was holding a book, whose title was too small to read. Getting out his magnifying glass, he saw that the book was *The Garden of Effort*.

My story or stories about the Place Dauphine followed. Claude responded with the obvious questions: what had become of her? had we ever met again? He mentioned that the manager or proprietor of the Hôtel Henri IV often ate in the restaurant where we were sitting, and that the hotel was still known for very inexpensive rooms. He then went across the square and returned with a card:

Hôtel Henri IV

25, Place Dauphine - 75001 Paris

Tout Confort - Prix Modérés

We crossed over to the Ile Saint Louis for a long, late lunch.

......

The shouts and screams of children playing in the courtyard of a nearby school, pouring in through the windows each day as I work in Irving's studio.

An event witnessed - a nonevent, invisible; the inversions and anachronisms; what was there is not, what was not, is; traces; "compressed into conflagration"; Titanium White; Zinc White.

The Arab Rider: Cobalt Blue and Delft Blue.

......

This evening at dinner, as I discuss the Denmark book with Dominique and Sandra, Dominique mentions a show that has just opened at the Beaubourg: *l'informe: mode d'emploi.*

......

Today, Irving and I review the last three can-
vases from the *Seine Series*.

Dominique and I meet later at the Beaubourg
to see the show. It is introduced by the quota-
tion from Bataille that I cite above ("A dictio-
nary would begin...").

......

First day of clear, hot weather since my
arrival. I walk to the offices of POL to sign cop-
ies of the French edition of *Sun* and to pick up
my copies.

......

On the 29th, the Dürer show with Dominique at the Petit Palais, then back to San Francisco to edit these notes.

......

Newspaper article after my return. Measurements taken at the sun's corona indicate that oxygen particles streaming from the sun in the solar wind are heated to more than 200 million degrees Fahrenheit, hotter than any temperature previously measured.

The readings focused on a point 310,000 miles above the edge of the solar disc. (A constant current of electrically charged gas issues from the sun, creating the solar wind. At 775,000 miles from the sun, the oxygen has accelerated to more than 500,000 miles per hour.)

......

Solstice fires, dancers leaping through the flames.

......

Tasseography: reading from the dregs left

in a cup.

......

These words on
parole.

K.W., *The Garden of Effort*

THE DANISH NOTEBOOK

....

A BRIEF NOTE

It does seem ironic that it was during the late stages of the COVID-19 lockdown that I was approached with the welcome thought of a new edition of *The Danish Notebook*, with its paratactic, deliberately haphazard record of wanderings and activities during a particularly nomadic period of my life. Would I be willing to provide an introductory note? A note on the *Notebook* then, from a certain distance, yet as well from an almost shocking emotional proximity, as the pages return me, to this self among others, self as at once same and other, far away and near.

Travels, the ebb and flow of a life at times "out of my hands." Memory vying with the immediate for primacy, occasionally overwhelming it. So perhaps a "surd map," as I speculate in the text, thinking of Robert Smithson. The folds of a life in transit: Prague, Brno, Paris, Copenhagen, Hawaii, et al, as noted and wondered at along the way? The then ongoing project with the Margaret Jenkins Dance Company of a text for dance, titled *Fault*, including all of its resonant meanings, at once psychological and physical, with the fraught, unstable politics of the moment, the fault-lines, the fractures, implicit. And travel at times with the dance company itself, here and there around the world as a selected poems is being readied for publication in Denmark. Form and formless engaged in their own seemingly irresolvable dynamic. And always the questions, "What do you see?" "What can you see?" Meaning also, of course, "What can you not see?" What lies within the folds, what hides in both the past and the present, who is this person taking notes along the way who seems not to know himself? And how do the dots connect, the dots both spatial and temporal, synchronic and diachronic? Does a pattern emerge in spite of itself? My age then

53, now 78, as we emerge cautiously and uncertainly from the shadow of plague. A life on the road, so recently unthinkable. Memory again, its truths and inventions.

To my astonishment while writing, the threads did gradually seem to connect, call out to others as if of their own will, "without a central logic." Was I (was the work) however obliquely, constructing something akin to a poetics, or the specter of one, a poetics without a program? A plot of sorts emerging, though far from what one finds in conventional narratives, fictional or otherwise?

Is there a Place Dauphine and was there ever? Can one "define" the sun anymore than one can define poetry? Are such questions for me to answer or for the reader, or neither? Is the unanswerable to be left in peace, in pieces? Some two and a half decades gone, with many friends in our shared arts, in that intimate, contentious company of makers, disappearing, the human company ever forming and reforming. Time and its intervals slipping away. Mean Solar Time tells us that the second is 1/86,400 of the mean solar day. So the sun and time, or is it the sun as time, Iselin, Jens, Claude?

Looking out now from this barn, which passes for a summer residence, I see the catalpas, the beetlebung, the mulberries, the Japanese maples, the hollies and firs, the white oaks, the needle pines, a witch hazel by the stone wall as the light descends. But what do I see? What do I prohibit myself from seeing, despite the commitment to an open text and, as possible, an open mind? And so it comes to a stop, lacking at the last a question mark:

> *What is submerged*
> *behind the liquid – flooded –*
> *eye*

Michael Palmer
2021

An American born in New York City and long resident of San Francisco, MICHAEL PALMER is the author, among many other books, of *Sun* (1988), *At Passages* (1995), *The Lion Bridge: Selected Poems 1972-1995* (1998), *The Promises of Glass* (2000), *Codes Appearing: Poems 1979-1988* (2001), *Company of Moths* (2005), *Thread* (2011), *The Laughter of the Sphinx* (2016), and most recently, *Little Elegies for Sister Satan* (2021). He is the translator of works by Emmanuel Hocquard, Vicente Huidobro, and Alexei Parshchikov, among others, and the editor of *Code of Signals: Recent Writings in Poetics* (1983). He is coeditor and co-translator of *Nothing the Sun Could Not Explain: 20 Contemporary Brazilian Poets* (1997, expanded edition, 2003). For over fifty years, he has also collaborated with the Margaret Jenkins Dance Company on numerous works.

NIGHTBOAT BOOKS

Nightboat Books, a nonprofit organization, seeks to develop audiences for writers whose work resists convention and transcends boundaries. We publish books rich with poignancy, intelligence, and risk. Please visit nightboat.org to learn about our titles and how you can support our future publications.

The following individuals have supported the publication of this book. We thank them for their generosity and commitment to the mission of Nightboat Books:

Kazim Ali
Anonymous (4)
Aviva Avnisan
Jean C. Ballantyne
The Robert C. Brooks Revocable Trust
Amanda Greenberger
Rachel Lithgow
Anne Marie Macari
Elizabeth Madans
Elizabeth Motika
Thomas Shardlow
Benjamin Taylor
Jerrie Whitfield & Richard Motika

This book is made possible, in part, by grants from the New York City Department of Cultural Affairs in partnership with the City Council, the New York State Council on the Arts Literature Program, and the Topanga Fund, which is dedicated to promoting the arts and literature of California.